The

Burning Skies

And

Rising Water

A

twin threat of heatwave and

flooding in America

Maddison Hussain

Disclaimer

This book may include repeated words and phrases. This is necessary for educational purposes, as it is to show that some important facts are clearly presented and emphasized. Repetition aids readers in comprehending the book and its contents, enhancing its readability and comprehensibility. The idea is to bring clarity and emphasis to specific points, which is especially useful for thorough understanding.

Table of content

INTRODUCTION

The goal of this book is to give a thorough examination of the status of climate change in the US as of now (2024), emphasizing its effects, patterns, and future predictions. It is critical to comprehend the complex impacts of climate change on different areas, people, and industries around the country as it continues to affect our environment. This paper attempts to clarify the real consequences of climate change, educate readers on its scientific foundation, and emphasize how urgently mitigation and adaptation actions must be undertaken.

Examining these patterns and anomalies will help us to understand how the climate is changing. The growing temperatures, altered precipitation patterns, and increased frequency of severe weather occurrences will be covered in detail in this book. Recognizing the wider effects of climate change on ecosystems, human health, and economic stability requires knowledge of these trends.

We explore past climate data as well as forecasts for the future. Past climate data allow us to follow the development of climate change throughout time and comprehend its long-term effects. For setting current conditions in context and predicting future events, this historical viewpoint is priceless. Models of climate change offer an insight into the future by simulating possible future situations depending on various greenhouse gas emission routes.

The highlighting of the differences in the effects of climate change across regions. Different climatic zones that each feel the consequences of climate change differently define the United States. For example, while the Southwest struggles with extreme droughts and water shortages, the Northeast experiences more precipitation and flooding. Whereas the Midwest struggles with both heatwaves and excessive rains, coastal areas are especially susceptible to hurricanes and sea level rise. Through an emphasis on these regional variations, the report seeks to offer a complex picture of climate change that acknowledges the different vulnerabilities and adaptation requirements found throughout the nation.

In looking at how climate change affects society and the economy. Economic ramifications of the growing frequency and intensity of extreme weather events include expenses associated with disaster response, infrastructure restoration, and interruptions to agriculture and industry. Moreover, socioeconomic inequality is made worse by climate change, which disproportionately affects weaker groups who are unable to adequately prepare for or recover from its effects.

The value of plans for adaptation and mitigation.
Mitigation measures aim to slow down the rate of climate change primarily by reducing greenhouse gas emissions. Among these tactics are increasing energy efficiency, switching to renewable energy sources, and putting carbon pricing in place. Conversely, adaptation plans seek to strengthen infrastructure and

communities' ability to withstand the unavoidable effects of climate change. Some mitigation and adaptation strategies will be examined in this paper, along with successful case studies and creative solutions.

As climate change is a worldwide issue, coordinated action at all levels from individual behavior modifications to international policy accords is necessary. This book offers a comprehensive and understandable summary of the current status of climate change in the US, encouraging responsible action and collaborative solutions. This aim is to give you the information and resources you need for a sustainable future, regardless of the role you play as a policymaker, educator, student, or concerned citizen.

In summary, Through this comprehensive analysis, this book aims to educate, inform, and inspire action, emphasizing the urgent need for effective mitigation and adaptation strategies to address the pressing challenges of a changing climate.

Overview of Climate Change in the United States

With effects on every area and industry in the US, climate change has become a major problem. Average temperatures in the nation have increased noticeably since the beginning of the 20th century, the contiguous United States has warmed by around 1.8°F (1°C). Extreme weather events are increasing along with this warming trend, these include more frequent and intense heat waves, higher rains, extended droughts, and stronger hurricanes.

Impacts of climate change vary noticeably by region.

Increased precipitation and flooding are experienced in the Northeast, while more severe rainfall events in the Midwest lead to more frequent flash floods. In contrast, the Western United States struggles with extreme droughts that endanger agriculture, water supplies, and raise the danger of wildfires. Rising sea levels worsen coastal erosion and floods, especially in the Gulf of Mexico and along the Atlantic coast.

Extreme weather change causes significant expenditures for economic disruption, infrastructure maintenance, and catastrophe response. Because shifting weather patterns impact crop production and livestock health, agriculture is especially vulnerable. Because they lack the means to either prepare for or recover from climatic catastrophes, vulnerable communities frequently suffer the most from these effects, which worsens social inequality.

The US is looking for ways to adapt and mitigate these issues. Through the use of renewable energy, energy efficiency enhancements, and carbon price schemes, mitigation measures aim to lower greenhouse gas emissions. By funding early warning systems, infrastructure, and natural remedies like wetland restoration, adaptation plans seek to increase resilience.

All things considered, climate change is significantly changing the ecology, economy, and society of the United States.

CHAPTER 1

Climate Change In The United States

General Climate Trends

Climate change is causing a variety of changes in environmental patterns in the United States, which has a big effect on the country's ecosystems, economy, and public health. The primary trends include rising temperatures, altered precipitation patterns, a rise in the frequency and intensity of extreme weather events, and rising sea levels. Understanding these trends is essential to understanding the broader effects of climate change and developing effective adaptation and mitigation strategies.

I. **Rise in temperature:** Over the past century, the average temperature in the contiguous United States has risen by roughly 1.8°F (1°C). While this warming trend is being felt in all locations, some are more affected than others, such as the Southwest and the Arctic. Temperatures have risen rapidly, especially in Alaska, as much as 4°F (2.2°C) in certain places since the 1960s. Because of this quick warming, Alaska's permafrost is thawing, there is less sea ice, and local ecosystems and communities are being negatively impacted.

Notable increases in temperature have also been noted in the lower 48 states of the Southwestern United States. Cities like Phoenix and Las

Vegas frequently see summer highs above 100°F (38°C), and heatwaves are becoming more frequent and intense. These extreme temperatures are linked to serious health risks, particularly for susceptible populations like children, the elderly, and those with underlying medical conditions.

II.   Modified   Precipitation   Patterns: Precipitation patterns have changed as a result of climate change, causing some regions to have higher rainfall and others to experience longer droughts. The Northeast and Midwest have seen a rise in the frequency of heavy precipitation events. For instance, precipitation dropped in the strongest 1% of storms increased by 42% in the Midwest and 55% in the Northeast during the 1950s. These times of intense rain can lead to flash floods, which can cause fatalities, major property damage, and the destruction of infrastructure.

Conversely, the Western United States is seeing more frequent and severe droughts. There has been a persistent drought in the Colorado River Basin, which supplies millions of people with clean water. This has limited the amount of water available for agriculture, industry, and urban areas. Severe droughts have increased the risk of wildfires, reduced agricultural production, and created a lack of water, especially in California. Elevated temperatures intensify the drought conditions by augmenting evaporation rates and diminishing snowpack levels, a vital water source for the region.

III. Rise in the intensity and frequency of extreme weather patterns: In the United States, extreme weather patterns including hurricanes, tornadoes, and wildfires have become more frequent and severe. Hurricanes are fueled by increased energy from increasing ocean temperatures, which produces storms with stronger winds and more rainfall. During the Atlantic hurricane season, there has been an increase in the activity of Category 4 and 5 storms. For example, the three big hurricanes that made landfall in 2017 (Harvey, Irma, and Maria) left behind significant damage and raised awareness of the growing threat that these powerful storms pose.

Furthermore, wildfires have become more frequent and severe, particularly in the West of the country. Longer fire seasons, higher temperatures, and higher fuel loads due to pest infestations and drought all raise the risk of wildfires. California has recently seen devastating wildfires that have resulted in significant property destruction, fatalities, and financial hardship. These fires have long-term repercussions on the environment, such as habitat loss, declining air quality, and increased carbon emissions.

IV. Rising Ocean Levels: Rising sea levels are another significant consequence of climate change, brought on by the melting of polar ice sheets and glaciers as well as the thermal expansion of heated seawater. The sea level has risen by 8 to 9 inches (21 to 24 cm) since the late 19th century, and the rate of rise has increased recently. The effects of rising sea levels are being felt more acutely by American coastal towns, particularly those close to the Atlantic and Gulf of Mexico coasts.

Cities like Miami, New York, and New Orleans are increasingly at risk from storm surges, high tides, and recurring floods. Coastal erosion and seawater intrusion into freshwater supplies are other major issues. The financial and social costs of adapting to increasing sea levels will be high, making investments in solid infrastructure and community planning necessary. The implementation of controlled retreat plans, the construction of seawalls, and the restoration of wetlands are crucial components of adaptation strategies for these vulnerable coastal districts.

V. Impacts On Society And The Economy: There are substantial economic implications to these climatic patterns. Particularly susceptible is agriculture, a vital sector of the US economy. Changing weather patterns have an impact on crop productivity and animal health. Drought-prone regions put water-intensive crops like cotton and almonds at risk. The overall productivity of American agriculture is increasingly under risk due to the unpredictable nature of weather patterns and shifting climatic conditions.

Human health is one more area where climate change has a significant effect. Two direct health risks linked to heatwaves are heat exhaustion and heatstroke. Increased temperatures also contribute to the production of ground-level ozone, a significant component of smog that exacerbates respiratory conditions like asthma. The transmission of infectious diseases is impacted by climate change as well. Warmer temperatures expand the habitats of vectors such as mosquitoes and ticks, which raises the risk of diseases including West Nile virus and Lyme disease.

The social aspects of climate change are equally significant. Because they lack the resources to adequately prepare for or recover from catastrophic weather events, marginalized and vulnerable people are often the ones that bear the brunt of climate repercussions. People are being forced to relocate increasingly frequently due to rising sea levels, hurricanes, and wildfires, disturbing local communities and widening socioeconomic disparity. To address these problems and provide equitable solution and adaptation strategies, coordinated actions are required.

Historical Climate Data And Predictions

A thorough analysis of past climate data and the projections produced by cutting-edge climate models is necessary to comprehend the trajectory of climate change in the United States. This strategy offers insightful information about previous patterns, present circumstances, and potential future events, facilitating improved preparation and reaction to the complex issues raised by climate change.

I. Historical Climate Records: Organizations such as the National Oceanic and Atmospheric Administration (NOAA) and the National Aeronautics and Space Administration (NASA) have painstakingly accumulated historical climate data in the United States, which clearly shows a warming trend over the past century. Since the turn of the 20th century, the average temperature in the contiguous United States has increased by around 1.8°F (1°C). This warming has not happened consistently; rather, it has happened in spurts, impacted by both human activity and natural variability.

Temperatures were comparatively constant in the early 20th century. But starting in the 1970s, the rate of warming sharply increased. This acceleration is accompanied by a discernible rise in greenhouse gas emissions from energy production, transportation, and industry. Well-established research links the observed warming to rising atmospheric quantities of carbon dioxide (CO_2) and other greenhouse gasses, highlighting the role of human activity in causing climate change.

Historical data show notable changes in precipitation patterns in conjunction to temperature rises. For instance, there has been an increase in the frequency and severity of heavy rainfall events in the Midwest and Northeast. Since the 1950s, the Midwest has had a 42% rise in precipitation dropping in the heaviest 1% of storms, while the Northeast has seen a 55% increase. These alterations make floods more common and severe, which puts a strain on emergency response and infrastructure systems.

On the other hand, precipitation overall has decreased in the Western United States, worsening the drought conditions. Long-lasting droughts have affected the Colorado River Basin, a vital source of water for millions of people, and have an effect on the availability of water for metropolitan areas, industry, and agriculture. In particular, California has seen catastrophic droughts that have increased the risk of wildfires and had a major negative impact on the environment and economy.

A further important component of historical climate data is sea level increase. Global sea levels have increased by around 8–9 inches (21–24 cm) since the late 19th century, and in recent decades, the rate of rise has accelerated. The melting of glaciers and ice sheets as well as the thermal expansion of warming saltwater are the main causes of this rise. The United States' coastal regions—especially those in the Atlantic and Gulf of Mexico—are seeing faster rates of sea level rise, which is causing more erosion and floods.

II. Forecasts For The Climate: Scientists utilize climate models, which simulate the interplay of the atmosphere, oceans, land surface, and ice, to estimate future climate conditions. These models, which present scenarios based on various paths for greenhouse gas emissions, were created by organizations like the Intergovernmental Panel on Climate Change (IPCC). The scenarios vary from high-emission pathways where emissions rise unabated to low-emission pathways where considerable efforts are made to minimize emissions.

III. Low-Pollution Routes: Future climate change may be considerably mitigated in situations in which considerable efforts are undertaken to cut greenhouse gas emissions. These scenarios usually presuppose a widespread switch to renewable energy sources, improved energy efficiency, and the adoption of laws like those pertaining to carbon pricing and reforestation. By the end of the twenty-first century, global temperatures are predicted to increase by roughly 2.7°F (1.5°C) to 3.6°F

(2°C) over pre-industrial levels under these scenarios.

Compared to high-emission scenarios, a low-emission pathway might moderate temperature increases in the United States and have less severe effects. But even in these hopeful scenarios, there will inevitably be some warming and related climatic impacts. For example, although the severity and frequency of extreme weather events would be lower than in high-emission scenarios, the incidence of extreme weather events, such as heatwaves and heavy rains, would still be greater than historical norms. A slower pace of sea level rise would also occur, lowering the possibility of catastrophic coastal erosion and flooding.

IV. High-Pollution Routes: The predictions are worse under high-emission scenarios, which occur when present trends in greenhouse gas emissions persist in the absence of major mitigation measures. By the 21st century, there might be a 6.3°F (3.5°C) to 8.1°F (4.5°C) increase in global temperatures over pre-industrial levels. The effects of such a rise would be severe and pervasive, affecting economies, human health, and ecosystems.

High-emission routes in the US would cause significant temperature increases in every region. For example, summer temperatures in some regions of the Southwest can frequently reach over 110°F (43°C), which increases the risk of outdoor activities and puts a tremendous load on energy systems because of the increased need for air conditioning. There would be more heavy rainfall events in the Northeast and Midwest going forward, which would increase the danger of flooding and overload stormwater management systems.

Regional Climate Predictions

The regional climatic prediction as follows:

I. Northeast: It is anticipated that the Northeast will see warmer winters and more precipitation. Under high emission scenarios, average winter temperatures could rise by 6°F to 8°F (3.3°C to 4.4°C) by the late 21st century. Infrastructure and ecosystems may be impacted by this warming if the snow season is shorter and winter storms occur more frequently.

II. Midwest: Greater frequency and intensity of heavy rainfall events are expected to occur in the Midwest, which will lead to an increase in the frequency of flooding. Under high-emission scenarios, average summer temperatures might climb by 7°F to 9°F (3.9°C to 5°C), making heatwaves more severe and putting strain on agricultural systems.

III. Southeast: Heatwaves can become more intense in the Southeast due to its susceptibility to rising temperatures and higher humidity. Stronger hurricanes and increasing sea levels, which endanger coastal infrastructure and residents, are further threats to the region.

IV. Southwest: Prolonged droughts and rising temperatures pose serious threats to the Southwest. Under high-emission scenarios, average summer temperatures would increase by 8°F to 10°F (4.4°C to 5.6°C) by the end of the century, with dire consequences for water supplies, agriculture, and wildfire risk.

V. West Coast: It is anticipated that there will be more frequent droughts and warmer temperatures throughout the West Coast, especially in California. The hotter and drier weather will enhance the risk of wildfires.

Coastal erosion and rising sea levels will also be problems for coastal areas.

VI. Alaska: Under high-emission scenarios, temperatures there are expected to rise by 8°F to 10°F (4.4°C to 5.6°C) by the late 21st century, indicating that the state would continue to undergo fast warming. Sea ice will continue to recede as a result of this warming, which will accelerate the thawing of permafrost and affect ecosystems and infrastructure.

2. Effects on infrastructure and human health: The United States' infrastructure and public health will be significantly impacted by the anticipated changes in the environment. Heat exhaustion and heatstroke are two direct health dangers associated with rising temperatures and heatwaves. Higher temperatures can also make air quality problems worse, which can worsen respiratory disorders.

Extreme weather occurrences will also put more demand on infrastructure. Because storms, flooding, and heatwaves are occurring more frequently and with greater severity, roads, bridges, and structures built for earlier climate conditions might not be able to sustain them. Infrastructure investments that are strong and built to withstand these new circumstances are crucial for maintaining both economic stability and public safety.

3. Financial Consequences: The effects of climate change on the economy are extensive. Severe weather conditions have the potential to destroy supply systems, reduce productivity, and cost billions of dollars in damages. Agriculture is especially vulnerable because agricultural output and livestock health are impacted by shifting weather patterns. Almonds and rice are two examples of water-intensive crops that may become less viable in drought-prone locations.

Adaptation and mitigation initiatives come at a high cost. Significant financial resources will be needed for the construction of renewable energy infrastructure, energy-efficient building retrofits, and coastal region protection against sea level rise. Nonetheless, in order to lower the long-term expenses and dangers related to climate change, these expenditures are required.

In summary

In conclusion, past climate data and projected future temperatures demonstrate the significant effects of climate change on the US. Extreme weather events are occurring more frequently, precipitation patterns have changed, and the nation is warming significantly. Coastal communities are facing a serious threat due to the increasing sea levels. Given the significant consequences of climate change to the economy, society, and environment, immediate action is required to reduce greenhouse gas emissions and prepare for the changing climate. In the face of these obstacles, the United States can create a more resilient and sustainable future by coordinating efforts at the local, state, and federal levels.

CHAPTER 2

Heatwaves in the United States

The Meaning and Features of Heatwaves

Prolonged periods of unusually hot weather, sometimes with considerable humidity, are known as heatwaves. A heatwave is generally described as a period of at least three consecutive days where temperatures surpass the average maximum temperature by a large margin, usually by 9°F (5°C) or more.

The precise threshold for what qualifies as a heatwave varies depending on the region. Although these occurrences can happen at any time of the year, summertime, when temperatures are already high, is when they happen most frequently.

Some Distinguishing Characteristics Of Heatwaves

I. High Temperature: Daytime highs during a heatwave frequently surpass typical averages. Additionally, nighttime temperatures can continue to be abnormally high, offering no respite from the heat of the day.
Heat Waves usually last a few days to a week, but in exceptional cases, they might linger for several weeks.

II. Humidity: High humidity often coexists with heatwaves in many areas, intensifying the sensation of heat and raising the possibility of heat-related illnesses. But low-humidity dry heat waves can also happen and are very dangerous, especially in arid areas.

III. Geographical Extent: Heatwaves have the capacity to hit several states or regions at once and to cover wide territories. A heatwave can differ greatly in its scope and intensity, with certain regions facing more extreme temperatures than others.

IV. Metropolitan Heat Island Effect: Because concrete, asphalt, and buildings absorb and hold heat more than natural landscapes, metropolitan areas are more likely to experience severe heat waves.

V. Reasons And Involving Elements;
Heatwave frequency and intensity are
influenced by a number of variables, such as air

conditions, human-caused climate change, and natural climatic variability.

Variability in natural climate are:

I. El Niño and La Niña: These cyclical fluctuations in Pacific Ocean sea surface temperatures have the potential to impact worldwide meteorological patterns. Particularly, El Niño occurrences are frequently linked to warmer and drier weather in several US regions.

II. Patterns of the Jet Stream: Heatwave generation and persistence can be influenced by the jet stream's position and strength. Heatwaves can occur when the jet stream gets "stuck" in a certain pattern, resulting in extended intervals of high pressure and clear skies.

Changes In Climate Caused By Humans are as follows:

I. Greenhouse Gas Emissions: The earth is warming overall as a result of an increase in greenhouse gasses like carbon dioxide and methane. Heatwaves are becoming more frequent and stronger due to global warming.

II. Urbanization: The growth of metropolitan regions raises local temperatures due to infrastructure and human activity. This phenomenon is known as the "urban heat island effect.

Particular Air Conditions

High-Pressure Systems: High-pressure systems, which produce clear sky, strong solar radiation, and stable air conditions, are frequently linked to heatwaves. By preventing precipitation and clouds from forming, these systems allow temperatures to rise sharply.

Subtropical Highs: Over the subtropical waters lie these semi-permanent systems of high pressure. They can bring protracted hot, dry weather when they travel across land.

Effects on Human Health and the Environment

Heatwaves can have a wide range of effects on the environment, public health, and the economy.

Effects on the Environment

I. Wildfires: During heatwaves, high temperatures and dry environments can cause wildfires to occur more often. The flammability of vegetation increases, and tiny sources of ignition have the potential to spark massive, destructive fires.

II. Water Resources: Heatwaves have the potential to worsen drought conditions, lowering the amount of water available for household, industrial, and agricultural usage. Increased temperature can also cause rivers and reservoirs to evaporate more quickly.

III. Agriculture: Heat stress can affect cattle and crops. Lower animal yields and higher livestock death rates can have a big financial impact on the agriculture industry.

IV. Ecosystems: Stressing out plants and animals can cause changes in the distribution of species and even damage to delicate habitats. This is how heat waves can change an ecosystem.

Effects on human health

Extended exposure to high temperature can result in the development of heat-related ailments, including dehydration, heatstroke, and exhaustion. Particularly for vulnerable groups including the elderly, young children, and individuals with underlying medical issues, these conditions may be fatal.

I. Cardiovascular and Respiratory Problems: Warm weather can make respiratory and cardiovascular conditions worse. Hospital admissions and death rates are known to rise during heatwaves.

II. Mental Health: Anxiety, depression, and other mental health conditions can be exacerbated by the stress and suffering that comes with intense heat.

III.Air Quality: Bad air quality frequently occurs during heatwaves. Elevated temperatures have the potential to enhance the production of ground-level ozone, a detrimental gas that exacerbates asthma and other respiratory disorders.

Heatwaves raise the energy needed for air conditioning, which puts a strain on power systems and increases the risk of power outages. Customers that use more energy also pay more for their electricity bills.

High temperatures have been shown to lower productivity, especially in outside jobs like construction and agriculture. It may also have an impact on interior workspaces lacking sufficient cooling systems.

I. Healthcare expenses: During heatwaves, hospital admissions and heat-related ailments are more common, which drives up healthcare expenses

Case Studies

1. Arizona Heatwave 2023 : One of the worst heat waves to ever hit Arizona occurred in June

2023. Phoenix had temperatures as high as 118°F (47.8°C), breaking existing records and putting a strain on the area's resources and infrastructure.

Characteristic And Impact

I. Record Temperature: Phoenix had several days with highs above 115°F (46.1°C), which resulted in a large number of heat-related illnesses and fatalities.

II. Energy Demand: As more people relied on air cooling, there was an increase in the demand for power. In certain places, the electricity grid was unable to keep up, resulting in rolling blackouts.

III. Wildfires: Numerous sizable wildfires that caused home destruction and prompted evacuations were fueled by the intense heat and dry weather.

IV. Droughts: Water shortages resulted from the extreme heat making drought conditions worse, lowering reservoir water levels and impacting water supplies.

Measures of Response

The city of Phoenix established a number of cooling centers to help residents who didn't have access to air conditioning.

Authorities started public health campaigns to inform the public about the risks associated with heat exposure and safe ways to stay cool.

I. Emergency Services: In preparation for heat-related emergencies, emergency services personnel and resources were heightened and on high alert.

2. Heatwave in California 2022: California saw a severe heatwave in September 2022 that devastated most of the state, including big cities like Los Angeles and San Francisco.

Characteristic And Impact

I. High Temperatures: Inland regions experienced highs of 115°F (46.1°C) while Los Angeles reached 110°F (43.3°C).

II. Energy Crisis: The heatwave increased demand for electricity, which put stress on the power system and forced planned blackouts to stop widespread disruptions.

California suffered severe agricultural losses as a result of the intense heat, including substantial losses in tomatoes, grapes, and almonds. Heat stress also negatively impacted livestock's health and output.

III. Wildfire: The extreme heat made the conditions perfect for wildfire. There were other significant fires that started, such as the Fairview wildfire that damaged many homes and scorched hundreds of acres.

Measures Of Response

California issued a proclamation of emergency in order to gather resources and assist impacted communities.

I. Public cooling facilities: In an effort to aid locals, especially the weaker segments of society, cities all around California established cooling centers.

II. Water Conservation Measures: In response to the prolonged drought, officials enforced stringent measures to conserve the diminishing water resources.

Recent Heatwave Incidents in 2024

The United States saw multiple notable heatwaves in the summer of 2024, highlighting the rising frequency and intensity of these occurrences.

I. The Northeast Heatwave: The temperature surpassed 100°F (37.8°C) for multiple days in cities like New York and Boston.

Hospitals saw a high rise in heat-related ailments, and public health advisories were released to advise people to stay inside and drink plenty of water.

Transportation infrastructure was put under stress by the heatwave, causing roads and bridges to swell and buckle from the extreme heat.

II. The Midwest Heatwave

Illinois, Missouri, and Ohio were hit by temperatures as high as 105°F (40.6°C) across the Midwest.

The heatwave that struck during the vital growth season caused serious harm to crops like soybeans and corn. Increased rates of mortality among cattle and poultry were also observed by livestock farmers.

Increased demand for electricity caused power disruptions in a number of cities, worsening the effects of the heatwave on locals.

III. The Southwestern Heatwave

A protracted heatwave with consistent highs above 110°F (43.3°C) hit the Southwest, encompassing Arizona, Nevada, and New Mexico.

The heatwave added to the region's already limited water supplies, which affected urban and agricultural water use.

The risk of wildfires was increased by the intense heat and dry weather, resulting in multiple large-scale fires that threatened towns.

In summary

In the US, heatwaves are becoming a bigger problem due to both human-caused climate change and inherent climatic unpredictability. There are serious hazards to the economy, the environment, and public health associated with these extreme weather events. Recognizing the traits, causes and impacts of heatwaves is crucial for developing effective response strategies and mitigating their effects. The following sections delve deeper into notable case studies from recent years, highlighting the specific challenges and responses associated with each event.

CHAPTER 3

Flooding In The United States

Definition And Types of Flooding

Flooding is the overflow of water onto normally dry land, which can occur due to various natural and man-made factors. Floods are among the most common and destructive natural disasters in the United States, causing extensive damage to property, infrastructure, and ecosystems, and posing significant risks to human life. Floods can be classified into several types, each with distinct characteristics and causes.

I. Riverine Flooding: Also known as fluvial flooding, this occurs when rivers overflow their banks due to excessive rainfall, rapid snowmelt, or ice jams. Riverine floods can develop slowly over several days or weeks (slow-rise floods) or rapidly with little warning (flash floods).

II. Flash Flooding: These floods develop quickly, often within minutes to hours of heavy rainfall, dam breaks, or sudden releases of water. Flash floods are characterized by their rapid onset and high velocity, making them particularly dangerous and difficult to predict.

III. Coastal Flooding: Coastal flooding happens when storm surges, high tides, or heavy rainfall associated with coastal storms (such as hurricanes and nor'easters) push seawater onto land. The combined effect of high tides and storm surges can exacerbate coastal flooding, leading to widespread inundation of low-lying coastal areas.

IV Urban Flooding: Urban flooding occurs in developed areas where impervious surfaces (like roads, sidewalks, and buildings) prevent water from infiltrating the ground. Heavy rainfall can overwhelm drainage systems, causing water to accumulate rapidly and flood streets, homes, and businesses.

V. Pluvial Flooding: This type of flooding is caused by extreme rainfall that generates surface runoff, which exceeds the capacity of local drainage systems. Pluvial floods can occur in both urban and rural areas and do not necessarily require proximity to rivers or coastlines.

VI.Groundwater Flooding: Groundwater flooding happens when the water table rises to the surface level due to prolonged rainfall or other hydrological factors. This type of flooding is less common but can be persistent and challenging to manage.

Causes And Contributing Factors

Flooding can result from a variety of natural and anthropogenic factors, often acting in combination. Understanding these causes is crucial for effective flood management and mitigation.

I. Heavy rainfall: Intense and prolonged rainfall is the primary cause of most floods. When the amount of rainfall exceeds the absorption capacity of the soil and the drainage capacity of rivers and streams, flooding occurs.

II. Snowmelt: Rapid melting of snow, particularly in the spring, can contribute to flooding in regions with significant snowfall.

Snowmelt adds large volumes of water to rivers and streams, increasing the risk of overflow.

III. Storm surges: Coastal areas are particularly vulnerable to storm surges, which occur when strong winds from hurricanes or other storms push seawater onto land. The impact is often exacerbated by high tides.

IV. Topography: The geographical features of an area, such as low-lying regions, floodplains, and valleys, can influence flood risk. Areas with poor drainage or steep slopes can experience more severe flooding.

V. Soil saturation: When the soil is already saturated from previous rainfall, additional rain has nowhere to go, leading to surface runoff and flooding. Soil type and land use practices also affect soil saturation levels.

VI. Urbanization: The development of urban areas with impervious surfaces reduces the land's natural ability to absorb water. As a result, more runoff is generated during rainstorms, increasing the risk of urban flooding.

VII. Climate change: Climate change is contributing to more frequent and intense rainfall events, rising sea levels, and more powerful storms, all of which exacerbate flooding risks. Warmer temperatures also lead to faster snowmelt and more frequent extreme weather events.

VIII. Human activities: Activities such as deforestation, land use changes, and poor watershed management can increase flood risk by altering natural water flow patterns and reducing the land's ability to absorb and slow down water.

Effects on infrastructure and the environment

Flooding affects infrastructure and the environment profoundly and in many ways, with major social, economic, and ecological repercussions.

Effects on the Environment

I. Ecosystem Disruption: By shifting the distribution of plant and animal species, floods have the power to modify ecosystems. Terrestrial habitats may be flooded and harmed, whereas aquatic habitats can be momentarily extended.

II. Water Quality: Pollutants including sewage, industrial chemicals, and agricultural runoff are frequently carried by floodwaters, contaminating bodies of water and endangering aquatic life as well as human health. Flood-related sedimentation can affect habitat structures and water quality as well.

III. Erosion of Soil: Floodwaters have the power to erode soil, which causes rivers and streams to become sedimented and lose its productive topsoil. Both aquatic ecosystems and land quality may be harmed by this.

IV. Damage to Vegetation: Wetlands, forests, and crops are among the vegetation that floods can destroy or harm. Reduced carbon sequestration, increased erosion, and the loss of wildlife habitat can all result from this loss of vegetation.

Impacts On Infrastructure
I. Property Damage: Homes, companies, and other structures may sustain significant damage from flooding, necessitating expensive repairs and financial losses. Water has the power to destroy personal things, weaken foundations, and harm electrical systems.

II.   **Transportation   Disruptions**:   Roads, bridges, trains, and airports may be submerged by floodwaters, impeding emergency response operations   and   causing   disruptions   to transportation   networks.   Repairing   damaged infrastructure   might   take   weeks   or   months, which   hinders   economic   activity   and movement.

III. Utility Services: Sewerage, water supply, and power are just a few of the vital utilities that might be affected by flooding. Serious health hazards can be posed by power outages and contaminated water supplies, which can further hamper recovery operations.

IV. Economic Losses: Flooding has an effect on the economy that goes beyond the immediate destruction   of   infrastructure   and   property. Floods can cause interruptions to supply chains, enterprises, and agriculture, which can result in higher expenses, lost revenue, and long-term economic difficulties.

V. Public Health: There are several concerns associated with floods that could affect people's health, such as the spread of waterborne illnesses, exposure to dangerous chemicals, and a higher chance of getting hurt or drowned. Flooding's psychological effects, such as stress and trauma, can have an influence on mental health.

Case Studies

1. 2023 Atmospheric river flooding in california: A succession of atmospheric river events—long, narrow zones in the atmosphere that carry moisture from the tropics—caused significant flooding in California in the early months of 2023. Heavy rains delivered by these atmospheric rivers caused severe flooding throughout the state.

Characteristic and effects

I. Severe Rainfall: The atmospheric rivers deposited historic levels of precipitation across California, with several regions witnessing more than 20 inches (508 mm) of rain in a matter of days. The rivers and reservoirs were overflowing due to the heavy downpour.

II. Flooding: Towns and agricultural areas were submerged when major rivers, such as the Sacramento and San Joaquin, spilled their banks. Significant damage was done to farmlands, residences, and infrastructure by the flooding.

III. Landslides: In steep and mountainous areas, the intense rains caused landslides, which obstructed roadways and made flood response operations even more difficult.

IV. Evacuations: In order to provide temporary accommodation and support, thousands of residents were evacuated from flood-prone locations and emergency shelters were set up.

Safety Measures

I. Emergency Services: Rescue activities were organized by state and local emergency services, which also supplied impacted areas with supplies and helped stranded citizens.

II. Infrastructure For Flood Regulate: Tests were conducted on the levees and dams that currently regulate flooding. The necessity for infrastructure upgrades was brought to light by breaches and breakdowns in certain locations.

III. Public Information: To notify the public and promote prompt evacuations, authorities used social media as well as other channels to provide flood warnings and advisories.

2022 Arizona Monsoon Floods

Known for its dry climate, Arizona had extreme floods in 2022 as a result of a strong monsoon season. Heavy downpours delivered by the monsoon rains caused flash floods throughout the state.

Characteristic and effects

I. Abundant Rainfall: Monsoon storms produced brief but heavy downpours, with several inches of rain falling in a few hours in certain places. Flash floods were caused by the water building up so quickly.

II. Flash Flooding: There was a lot of flash flooding in urban areas, especially in Tucson and Phoenix. Roads become rivers, engulfing houses, companies, and automobiles.
Bridges, drainage systems, and roadways were all harmed by floodwaters. Roads that had

washed out momentarily cut off some rural settlements.

III. Emergency Responses: Due to rising waters, first responders had to perform multiple water rescues to free people stranded in cars and structures.

Safety Measures

I. Flash Flood Warnings: In order to alert the public to the impending risk and urge them to take safety precautions, the National Weather Service issued flash flood warnings and alerts.

II. Community Preparedness: To help impacted citizens, local governments activated emergency plans, set up shelters, and coordinated with relief organizations.

III. Post-Flood Recovery: Work concentrated on removing debris, fixing broken infrastructure, and helping displaced people get back to their houses.

Miami Hurricane Flooding And King Tides

King tides and storm surges brought on by hurricanes present special flooding challenges for Miami, Florida. King tides, the greatest anticipated high tides of the year, frequently occur in conjunction with strong winds and rainstorms, making urban flooding worse.

Characteristics and effects

I. **King tides**: Even on bright days, these naturally occurring tides can cause sea levels to momentarily surge, resulting in coastal flooding. Miami's streets and communities that are low to the ground are especially susceptible.

II. **Hurricane flooding**: Hurricanes, which bring powerful winds, rain, and storm surges, are prone to hitting Miami due to its location. Severe flooding can result from the combination of king tides and surges caused by hurricanes.

I. Infrastructure improvements: Miami has invested in infrastructure projects to combat flooding, including the installation of pumps, raising roads, and improving drainage systems. These measures aim to manage both tidal and stormwater flooding more effectively.

II. Flood barriers and seawalls: The city has been enhancing its coastal defenses by building and upgrading seawalls and flood barriers to protect against storm surges and high tides. These structures help to minimize the impact of floodwaters on vulnerable areas.

III. Public awareness campaigns: Miami has launched public awareness campaigns to educate residents about flood risks and encourage preparedness. This includes providing information on flood insurance, evacuation routes, and emergency plans.

IV. Evacuation planning: In anticipation of hurricanes, the city has developed detailed evacuation plans and shelters to ensure the safety of residents. These plans are regularly updated and tested through drills and simulations.

Recent 2024 Flood Incidents

The year 2024 saw several significant flood events across the United States, highlighting the growing challenge of managing and mitigating flood risks in the face of climate change and extreme weather patterns.

1. Northeast Flooding

I. Intense rainfall: In the summer of 2024, the Northeast experienced several severe storms that brought intense rainfall, resulting in widespread flooding. Cities such as New York and Boston saw significant inundation, with rainfall totals exceeding 10 inches (254 mm) in some areas over a short period.

II. Urban flooding: Urban areas, with their extensive impervious surfaces, were particularly hard hit. Streets and subways in New York City were flooded, disrupting transportation and causing extensive property damage.

III. Infrastructure strain: The aging infrastructure in many Northeast cities struggled to cope with the volume of water, leading to failures in drainage

Midwest flooding recovery efforts.

I. Spring Floods: The Midwest faced severe spring flooding due to a combination of heavy rainfall and rapid snowmelt. Rivers such as the Mississippi and Missouri overflowed, inundating farmlands and communities.

II. Agricultural Impact: The floods caused extensive damage to crops and livestock, exacerbating economic losses for farmers and impacting food supply chains. The agricultural sector faced challenges in both immediate recovery and long-term resilience planning.

III. Community Displacement: Many rural communities were temporarily displaced due to floodwaters, highlighting the need for better floodplain management and community support systems.

2. Southern flooding

I. Gulf Coast Storms: The Gulf Coast, including states like Louisiana and Texas, experienced multiple storms that brought heavy rainfall and storm surges. Cities like New Orleans and Houston were particularly affected, with significant flooding disrupting daily life.

II. Economic disruption: The flooding caused substantial economic disruption, impacting industries ranging from oil and gas to tourism. The recovery efforts focused on restoring infrastructure and supporting affected businesses.

Safety Efforts

In response to repeated flooding, Gulf Coast cities have been investing in resilience measures, such as improved levees, wetland restoration, and community-based adaptation projects.

In summary

Flooding remains one of the most pervasive and challenging natural disasters facing the United States. As climate change continues to influence weather patterns, the frequency and severity of floods are expected to increase, posing significant risks to communities, infrastructure, and ecosystems.

Understanding the different types of flooding, their causes, and their impacts is essential for developing effective mitigation and response strategies. The case studies of recent flood events in California, Arizona, Miami, and other regions illustrate the diverse challenges posed by flooding and the importance of proactive measures to enhance resilience.

Investments in infrastructure improvements, public awareness campaigns, and community-based adaptation efforts are crucial for mitigating the impacts of flooding and protecting vulnerable populations. By learning from past events and leveraging scientific advancements, the United States can better prepare for future floods and build a more resilient and sustainable future.

CHAPTER 4

Interconnection Between Heat Waves And Flooding

Hardening Of Soils And Runoff Processes

When the top layer of soil dries up and compacts due to intense heat, it is referred to as soil crusting or hardening. This process is especially problematic in regions that endure protracted heat waves because the frequent exposure to high temperatures and drying out of the soil exacerbates its incapacity to absorb water.

1. Mechanisms Of Hardening Soil

I. Moisture Loss: As water evaporates from the soil's surface during a heatwave, the soil's moisture content rapidly drops. The soil particles become harder and shrink due to this drying process, forming a crusty layer that is less porous.

Long-term high temperatures have the potential to break down organic matter and modify the structure of soil through chemical changes. As a result, the soil surface becomes denser and less porous.

II. Loss of vegetations: Heat waves have the potential to cause a large amount of dying or wilting of plants. Without vegetation roots, the soil gets more compacted; their presence helps to keep the soil loose and porous.

2. Effect Of Runoff

I. Decreased Infiltration: Soil loses its capacity to absorb water when it is hardened. Rainfall increases the chance of floods because it flows off the surface rather than into the soil.

II. Increased Surface Runoff: Because of the impermeable soil surface, there is more surface runoff, which can build up quickly and cause flash floods. Urban places are especially vulnerable because of their impermeable surfaces.

III. Erosion and Sedimentation: Sediment deposits in rivers and streams and severe soil erosion caused by increased runoff might occur. This sedimentation may lessen water channels' capacity, increasing the risk of flooding.

California as a case study

A clear illustration of how soil hardening can increase the risk of flooding is found in California. The state has seen extreme heat waves and droughts, which have been followed by periods of heavy rain.

I. Drought and heat waves: California has experienced extended drought conditions along with intense heat waves in recent years, which has caused a major hardening of the soil throughout the state.

II. Severe rainfall events: The hardened soil was unable to absorb the water when atmospheric river events brought intense rains in the early months of 2023. This led to extensive floods and quick runoff, especially in cities like Los Angeles and San Francisco.

III. Impact on agriculture: Heatwaves hardened the soil in the Central Valley, a significant agricultural region, and subsequent flooding caused crop losses and soil erosion.

3. Strategies for Mitigation

I. Soil management practices: By preserving soil moisture and structure, practices including mulching, cover crops, and the application of organic amendments can lessen the effects of soil hardening.

II. Restoration of vegetation: Replanting vegetation, particularly deeply rooted plants, can enhance water infiltration and soil structure. This can lessen the chance of flooding and manage drainage.

III. Infrastructure adaptation: Installing rain gardens, green roofs, and permeable pavements are a few ways to improve urban infrastructure to handle more runoff, absorb excess water, and avoid flooding.

Heat Waves Effect on Weather Patterns

Heatwaves have a big impact on weather patterns, which can create situations that make flooding more likely. Prolonged high heat waves have the potential to change atmospheric dynamics, which can affect how storms and precipitation events form and intensify.

Atmospheric Circulation Modification
Heat Waves have an impact on atmospheric circulation patterns, which can change how precipitation is distributed and how storm systems originate.

Influence Mechanisms

I. High-pressure systems: Heatwaves are frequently linked to enduring high-pressure systems that can permanently alter local weather patterns. These systems can obstruct the movement of low-pressure systems, leading to protracted dry environments followed by severe rains when the pattern shifts.

II. Jet stream alterations: Extreme heat can induce adjustments in the jet stream, (the fast-flowing air currents in the sky that impact weather patterns). Weather systems may be stopped due to changes in the jet stream, which raises the possibility of heavy and protracted precipitation.

III. Humidity and moisture transport: Heat waves cause more moisture to enter the atmosphere by increasing evaporation rates. The upcoming rainfall may be stronger due to this higher moisture content, which could result in more severe floods

Case Study

1. Northeast Floods In 2024

The Northeastern flooding incidents of 2024 serve as an example of how heat waves can alter weather patterns and raise the risk of flooding.

I. Extended Heatwave: In 2024, there was an extended heatwave in the Northeast that resulted in temperatures that were constantly over 90°F (32°C). As a result, a persistent high-pressure system developed over the area that persisted for several weeks.

II. Jet Stream Displacement: The extreme heat forced the jet stream to change direction, which stopped the meteorological pattern. Eventually, the high-pressure system moved, and a low-pressure system that produced significant rainfall took its place.

III. Heavy Rainfall: The prolonged heat wave combined with other climatic factors, such as elevated moisture levels, produced heavy and persistent rainfall. As a result, major cities like New York and Boston had significant flooding.

Effect on the Risk of Floods

I. Prolonged dry and raining periods: Changes in air circulation can cause long stretches of dry weather interspersed with intensely sudden rainfall. In the same area, this trend raises the risk of both flooding and drought.

Extreme Weather Events: Storms, hurricanes, and periods of intense rainfall may become more frequent and severe as a result of changes in atmospheric dynamics. Flood risks are raised by these occurrences' heightened frequency and intensity.

Compound Events: When several extreme weather events happen quickly after one another, it can be a result of the interaction between heat waves and modified weather patterns.

Infrastructure and emergency response systems may become overloaded as a result.

Creating systems that can survive harsh weather conditions is essential to building infrastructure to counter flooding and heat waves. This covers urban cooling solutions, drainage systems, and flood barriers.

In summary

Heatwaves and flooding are related, which emphasizes how complex climate risks are and how important it is to have comprehensive management plans. Heatwaves affect overall weather patterns and cause runoff dynamics to change, which in turn hardens the soil and increases the danger of flooding.Comprehending these associations is essential for formulating efficacious mitigation and adaptation strategies. Communities can strengthen their counter to heatwaves and flooding by tackling the underlying causes of climate change and putting integrated risk management strategies into place. This will protect people's lives, property, and ecosystems for future generations.

CHAPTER 5

Regional Focus And Specific Challenges

Southwestern United States

The Southwestern United States is known for its arid and semi-arid climate, which makes it particularly vulnerable to both heatwaves and flooding. The region includes states such as Arizona, California, Nevada, New Mexico, Utah, Colorado, and Texas. Each of these states faces unique challenges related to climate change, especially in terms of extreme heat and water management.

ARIZONA

1. Heatwave Incidents: Arizona frequently experiences some of the highest temperatures in the United States. Heatwaves are a common occurrence, especially in urban areas like Phoenix and Tucson.

I. Phoenix 2023 heatwave: In the summer of 2023, Phoenix experienced one of its most severe heat waves, with temperatures exceeding 110°F (43°C) for several days. This extreme heat strained the electrical grid, caused numerous heat-related illnesses, and resulted in several fatalities.

II. Impact on public health: The intense heat poses significant risks to public health, particularly for vulnerable populations such as the elderly, children, and those with pre-existing health conditions. Emergency rooms saw a sharp increase in patients suffering from heat exhaustion and heatstroke during the 2023 heatwave.

III. Urban heat island effect: Urban areas in Arizona are particularly susceptible to the urban heat island effect, where concrete and asphalt absorb and re-radiate heat, making cities significantly hotter than their rural surroundings. Efforts to mitigate this effect include planting trees, creating green spaces, and installing reflective roofing materials.

2. Flooding Incidents

Despite its arid climate, Arizona is prone to flash flooding, particularly during the monsoon season.

I. 2022 Monsoon floods: The summer of 2022 saw intense monsoon storms that brought heavy rainfall to Arizona, leading to significant flash flooding. Areas like Flagstaff and Scottsdale were particularly hard hit, with streets turning into rivers and homes being inundated.

II. Impact on infrastructure: Flash floods caused extensive damage to infrastructure, including roads, bridges, and drainage systems. The rapid accumulation of water overwhelmed urban drainage systems, leading to widespread flooding in several communities.

III. Community response: The state has invested in flood mitigation measures, such as improved drainage systems and flood control projects. Public awareness campaigns also educate residents on how to prepare for and respond to flash floods.

CALIFORNIA

1. Heatwave Incidents

California's diverse climate includes regions that regularly experience extreme heatwaves, particularly in inland areas.

I. 2022 Heatwave: In the summer of 2022, California faced a severe heatwave with temperatures soaring above 115°F (46°C) in some areas. This extreme heat led to increased electricity demand, resulting in rolling blackouts as the power grid struggled to cope.

II. Wildfire risk: Heatwaves in California are often accompanied by dry conditions, significantly increasing the risk of wildfires. The 2022 heatwave was followed by several large wildfires that caused widespread damage and evacuations.

III. Health impacts: The extreme heat posed serious health risks, with a notable increase in heat-related illnesses and deaths. Public health campaigns aimed to raise awareness about the dangers of heat and promote measures to stay cool and hydrated.

2. Flooding Incidents

California also faces significant flooding risks, particularly from atmospheric river events and flash floods.

I. Atmospheric River Flooding 2023: In early 2023, a series of atmospheric river events brought intense rainfall to California, leading to widespread flooding. Areas like Sacramento and the San Joaquin Valley experienced severe inundation, with rivers overflowing their banks.

II. infrastructure damage: The heavy rains caused extensive damage to infrastructure, including levees, roads, and homes. The state's old water management infrastructure was particularly vulnerable, highlighting the need for modernization.

III. Safety Measures: California has been investing in flood safety measures, such as levee reinforcement, wetland restoration, and improved forecasting and emergency response systems. These efforts aim to reduce the impact of future flooding events.

NEVADA

1. Heatwave Incidents

Nevada, with its desert climate, frequently experiences extreme heat, particularly in cities like Las Vegas.

I. Las Vegas 2023 heatwave

In 2023, Las Vegas endured a prolonged heat wave with temperatures reaching 115°F (46°C). This extreme heat led to increased energy consumption as residents relied heavily on air conditioning.

II. Tourism impact: The heatwave had a noticeable impact on tourism, as outdoor activities became dangerous during peak temperatures. Hotels and resorts implemented measures to protect tourists, such as providing cooling stations and promoting indoor activities.

III. Health risks: The extreme heat posed significant health risks, especially for the homeless population and outdoor workers. Emergency services were stretched thin responding to heat-related emergencies.

2. Flooding Incidents

Nevada is also susceptible to flash flooding, particularly in areas with dry, compacted soils that do not absorb water well.

I. 2022 flash floods: In 2022, parts of Nevada, including Reno and rural communities, experienced severe flash flooding following intense summer thunderstorms. The floods caused road closures and damage to homes and businesses.

II. Desert flooding : The arid landscape of Nevada means that heavy rainfall can quickly lead to flash flooding, as the dry soil has limited absorption capacity. This creates rapid runoff and sudden, dangerous flood conditions.

III. Mitigation Efforts: Efforts to mitigate flooding in Nevada include improving stormwater management systems and constructing flood control basins to capture and store runoff.

NEW MEXICO

1. Heatwave Incidents

New Mexico, with its high desert climate, frequently experiences extreme heat, particularly in the summer months.

I. 2023 Heatwave: In 2023, New Mexico saw one of its hottest summers on record, with temperatures regularly exceeding 100°F (38°C). This prolonged heat wave strained the state's water resources and agricultural sector.

II. Impact on agriculture: The extreme heat and dry conditions affected crop yields, particularly for water-intensive crops like chile peppers and pecans. Farmers had to adapt by employing more efficient irrigation techniques and selecting drought-resistant crops.

III. Public health: The heatwave led to an increase in heat-related illnesses, particularly among outdoor workers and vulnerable populations. Public health advisories and cooling centers were established to help mitigate the effects of the extreme heat.

1. Flooding Incidents

New Mexico is prone to flash flooding, especially during the monsoon season when heavy rains can lead to rapid runoff.

I. 2022 Monsoon Floods: The monsoon season of 2022 brought heavy rains and flash flooding to parts of New Mexico, including Albuquerque and Santa Fe. The floods caused significant damage to homes and infrastructure.

II. Wildfire: Areas affected by wildfires are particularly vulnerable to flash floods, as the lack of vegetation increases runoff. This was evident in the aftermath of the Hermit's Peak/Calf Canyon Fire, where wildfire contributed to severe flooding.

3.Community Preparedness

The state has focused on improving flood preparedness and response, including enhancing early warning systems and promoting community awareness about flood risks.

UTAH

1. Heatwave Incidents

Utah experiences frequent heat waves, particularly in its desert and semi-arid regions.

I. 2023 Heatwave: The summer of 2023 saw Utah experiencing extended periods of extreme heat, with temperatures frequently exceeding 100°F (38°C) in cities like Salt Lake City and St. George. This heatwave put significant pressure on the state's water resources.

II. Impact on reservoirs: The extreme heat led to increased evaporation from reservoirs and lakes, exacerbating water shortages in an already arid state. This was particularly problematic for agricultural and municipal water supplies.

III.Public health concerns: The heatwave resulted in a surge of heat-related health issues, prompting the state to issue heat advisories and open cooling centers to help residents cope with the extreme temperatures.

2. Flooding Incidents

Utah is also susceptible to flash flooding, particularly in its mountainous and canyon regions.

I. 2022 Flash Floods: In 2022, heavy rains led to flash flooding in areas like Zion National Park and Moab. The floods caused significant damage to trails, roads, and tourist facilities, highlighting the vulnerability of popular outdoor recreation areas.

II. Canyon Flood Risks

Utah's unique geography, with its numerous canyons and slot canyons, makes it particularly vulnerable to flash floods. Visitors to these areas are often at risk, necessitating robust warning systems and visitor education.

III   Mitigation Efforts: Efforts to mitigate flood risks in Utah include improving flood forecasting, enhancing emergency response plans, and constructing flood control infrastructure in vulnerable areas.

COLORADO

1. Heatwave Incidents

Colorado experiences extreme heat, particularly in its lower elevation areas and urban centers.

I. Denver 2023 heatwave

The summer of 2023 saw Denver experiencing one of its hottest summers on record, with temperatures frequently exceeding 95°F (35°C). This heatwave strained the state's water and energy resources.

II. Agricultural Impacts: The extreme heat affected Colorado's agricultural sector, particularly crops like corn and wheat. Farmers faced challenges in irrigation and water management, leading to reduced yields.

III. Public health: The heatwave led to an increase in heat-related illnesses, prompting public health campaigns to promote hydration and the use of cooling centers.

2. Flooding Incidents

Colorado is prone to both riverine and flash flooding, particularly in areas affected by snowmelt and heavy summer storms.

I. 2022 Flash Floods: In 2022, Colorado experienced significant flash flooding in areas like Boulder and Fort Collins following intense summer thunderstorms. The floods caused damage to homes, businesses, and infrastructure.

II. Wildfire : Areas affected by wildfires, such as the Cameron Peak Fire, are particularly vulnerable to flooding. The lack of vegetation and altered soil conditions increase runoff and flood risks in these regions.

TEXAS

1. Heatwave Incidents

Texas experiences some of the most severe and prolonged heat waves in the United States, particularly in its southern and western regions.

I. 2023 Heatwave: In the summer of 2023, Texas experienced an intense heatwave with temperatures soaring above 110°F (43°C) in several areas, including Austin, San Antonio, and Dallas. The extreme heat led to increased demand for electricity, resulting in power outages in some regions.

II. Impact on agriculture: The agricultural sector in Texas was severely impacted by the heatwave, with crops such as cotton, corn, and wheat suffering from heat stress and this reduced their yields. Ranchers also faced challenges as water sources dried up and feed became scarce.

3. Public Health Concerns: The heatwave caused a significant rise in heat-related illnesses and deaths. Cities implemented emergency measures, such as opening cooling centers and distributing water to vulnerable populations.

2. Flooding Incidents

Texas is also highly susceptible to flooding, particularly from hurricanes, tropical storms, and heavy rainfall events.

I. Hurricane Harvey 2017: While it's not within the past couple of years, the effects of

Hurricane Harvey are still visible. The hurricane brought unprecedented rainfall to Houston and surrounding areas, resulting in catastrophic flooding. The disaster highlighted the vulnerability of Texas to extreme weather events and the need for improved flood management strategies.

II. 2022 floods: In 2022, parts of Texas, particularly along the Gulf Coast and in central Texas, experienced severe flooding due to heavy rainfall. Cities like Houston and San Antonio saw streets and homes inundated, causing widespread damage and displacements.

III. Infrastructure and response: Texas has been investing in flood mitigation infrastructure, such as reservoirs, levees, and improved drainage systems. The state also focuses on enhancing emergency response and community preparedness to better cope with future flood events.

Southeastern United States

The Southeastern United States, particularly states like Florida, faces unique challenges related to climate change, including sea level rise, hurricanes, and extreme weather events. Miami, in particular, is highly vulnerable to flooding from king tides and hurricanes.

FLORIDA (MIAMI)

1. Flooding Incidents From King Tides And Hurricanes

Miami is particularly vulnerable to flooding due to its low elevation, high water table, and proximity to the ocean. The city faces frequent flooding from both king tides and hurricanes, posing significant challenges to infrastructure, public health, and the economy.

King Tides

King tides, which are the highest high tides of the year, regularly cause flooding in Miami. These events are becoming more frequent and severe due to sea level rise. Streets in low-lying areas, such as Miami Beach and the financial district, often become submerged, disrupting daily life and business operations.

Hurricane Irma 2017

While it's not in the immediate past few years, Hurricane Irma in 2017 caused extensive flooding and damage in Miami. The storm surge inundated coastal areas, and the heavy rains led to widespread urban flooding. The aftermath of Irma underscored the city's vulnerability to extreme weather and the need for planning against any coming storm in the future.

2. 2024 Hurricane Season

The 2024 hurricane season saw Miami experience significant flooding from a series of storms. These events highlighted the ongoing threat of hurricanes and the challenges of managing flood risks in a changing climate.

I. Infrastructure And Adaptation: Miami has been investing heavily in infrastructure to combat flooding, including raising roads, installing pumps, and enhancing the stormwater drainage system. The city is also exploring innovative solutions such as building sea walls and creating green infrastructure to absorb and manage floodwaters.

II. Community Effort: Efforts to increase community resilience include public education campaigns about flood risks, the importance of flood insurance, and evacuation planning. Miami is also working on updating building codes and land-use planning to better prepare for future flood events.

In summary

The United States faces a diverse array of climate change-related challenges, with each region experiencing its unique set of impacts from heat waves and flooding. The Southwestern United States, including states like Arizona, California, Nevada, New Mexico, Utah, Colorado, and Texas, deals with extreme heat, prolonged droughts, and sudden flash floods. On the other hand, the Southeastern United States, particularly Florida, contends with rising sea levels, king tides, and the destructive force of hurricanes.

Understanding these regional specificities and the interplay between various climate risks is crucial for developing effective mitigation and adaptation strategies. By investing in infrastructure improvements, enhancing emergency response capabilities, these regions can better prepare for and respond to the challenges posed by a changing climate. Comprehensive and coordinated efforts at the local, state, and federal levels are essential to safeguard lives, property, and ecosystems from the growing threats of heatwaves and flooding.

CHAPTER 6

Detailed Analysis Of Major Heatwave And Flooding Events

California: 2023 Heatwave Leading To Flooding From Atmospheric Rivers

California, a state well-acquainted with extreme weather, experienced a series of calamitous events in 2023 that highlighted the dangerous interplay between heatwaves and subsequent flooding. The summer of 2023 was marked by one of the hottest periods on record, extending from early June to late August. Inland regions, such as the Central Valley, saw temperatures consistently exceed 110°F (43°C), and even the typically temperate coastal areas suffered from unusually high temperatures.

This extreme heat led to significant strain on California's electricity and water resources. The increased demand for air conditioning during the heatwave resulted in rolling blackouts in several areas. Water resources, already stretched thin due to a prolonged drought, were further depleted. The public health impacts were severe, with a notable rise in heat-related illnesses and fatalities. To mitigate these effects, cities established cooling centers and emergency services were on high alert, though they were often overwhelmed by the scale of the crisis.

In early September, just as the heatwave began to wane, California was hit by a series of atmospheric rivers. These atmospheric rivers, which are essentially narrow corridors of concentrated moisture, originated from the Pacific Ocean and brought intense, sustained rainfall to the state. Some areas received over 10 inches (25 cm) of rain within a few days, causing rivers and streams to overflow. The already parched and hardened soil, a result of the summer heatwave, could not absorb this sudden deluge, leading to rapid runoff and significant flooding.

The impact of this flooding was devastating. Urban areas such as Los Angeles, San Francisco, and Sacramento faced severe disruptions. Streets turned into rivers, homes and businesses were inundated, and transportation networks were severely affected. The Central Valley, a major agricultural hub, was particularly hard-hit, with floodwaters destroying crops, livestock, and infrastructure. The economic losses were substantial, with damages running into billions of dollars. Emergency response was swift but challenged by the scale of the disaster. Thousands of residents were evacuated, and the National Guard was deployed to assist with rescue operations and provide aid.

The 2023 events underscored the need for improved weather forecasting and early warning systems in California. Enhanced predictive models can help prepare for such compound events. Additionally, the state is investing in infrastructure resilience, including strengthening levees, improving drainage systems, and developing more robust water management strategies. Long-term climate adaptation strategies, such as restoring natural floodplains and wetlands, are also being pursued to help absorb floodwaters and mitigate the impact of such extreme weather events.

Arizona 2022: Monsoon Floods Following Extreme Heat

Arizona's climate is marked by intense heat and a distinct monsoon season, making the state especially vulnerable to severe weather occurrences. In 2022, Arizona saw a strong heatwave followed by intense monsoon rains, resulting in widespread flash floods.

The heatwave, which lasted from late May to early July, caused temperatures in locations such as Phoenix and Tucson to regularly reach 110°F (43°C). This protracted period of high heat dried out the soil and flora, leaving the state more vulnerable to future rainfall. The heatwave caused significant strain on the electrical grid and water supplies, resulting in power outages and water limitations. Hospitals have observed an upsurge in heat-related illnesses and mortality. The agricultural industry was also harmed, with crops wilting and production declining owing to heat and water scarcity.

The monsoon season began in mid-July with strong rainfall and thunderstorms. The dried and hardened soil was unable to absorb the quick rush of water, resulting in fast runoff and flash floods. Cities like Flagstaff and Scottsdale, as well as rural areas, were severely flooded. Rising waters wreaked havoc on roads, wrecked homes, and shut off some communities. Flooding caused significant property destruction and economic losses. Insurance claims increased dramatically, and many people faced lengthy recovery processes. Several people died, and more were displaced as emergency shelters were set up to help those impacted.

In response to these incidents, Arizona is investing in enhanced flood management systems, such as better drainage infrastructure and flood control techniques. Public awareness initiatives are underway to educate citizens about the dangers of flash floods and the significance of disaster preparedness. Furthermore, efforts are being made to improve vegetation and soil management practices in order to increase water absorption and reduce runoff after heavy rains.

New Mexico 2022 Post-Wildfire Flooding

In recent years, New Mexico has seen an increase in wildfire activity, which has resulted in significant flooding disasters. The 2022 monsoon season caused severe rainfall to areas recently damaged by wildfires, resulting in widespread flooding. Several big wildfires broke out in New Mexico during the spring and early summer of 2022, notably, the Hermit's Peak/Calf Canyon Fire. These fires ravaged vast regions of woodland and grassland, leaving behind unstable soil and ashes. The absence of vegetation, which typically serves to stabilize the soil and absorb rainfall, raised the risk of erosion and flood.

When the monsoon season came, the heavy rainfall in these wildfire-affected areas caused rapid runoff and flash flooding. The naked and burnt soil couldn't absorb the water, so floodwaters transported ash, debris, and sediment downstream, choking rivers and streams. Communities near burn scars, such as those in the Santa Fe National Forest, were severely flooded. Roads, bridges, and homes in flood-prone locations have been damaged or destroyed. The floodwaters also fouled water sources with ash and debris. The flooding resulted in considerable economic losses, particularly for rural towns that rely on agriculture and tourism. The recovery procedure was slow and expensive.

Several lives were lost, and many inhabitants were displaced as emergency services were overburdened, and shelters were established to aid those impacted. New Mexico is researching ways to address post-wildfire flood concerns, such as early warning systems and better land management practices. Efforts are continuing to recover plants in burned areas, which will help stabilize the soil and decrease erosion. Community preparedness initiatives are being created to educate residents on the dangers of post-wildfire floods and the significance of disaster planning.

Recent 2024 heatwave and flood incidents.

A number of extreme weather events have occurred across the United States in 2024, illustrating climate change's persistent impact on the frequency and intensity of heatwaves and floods. Throughout the summer of 2024, numerous locations endured record-breaking heatwaves, followed by severe flooding.

In the Southwestern United States, states such as Arizona, California, and Nevada were particularly badly struck by severe heatwaves. These heat waves lasted several weeks, with temperatures frequently topping 110°F (43°C). The severe heat raised electrical demand, causing power outages in some regions. Heat-related illnesses and mortality caused a pressure on public health systems. Crops wilted and water resources diminished, wreaking havoc on these states' agricultural economies.

As the summer proceeded, many areas saw a transition from intense heat to heavy rain. California, which is still healing from the 2023 atmospheric river occurrences, had another round of strong rainstorms. The rains forced rivers and streams to overflow, resulting in widespread flooding. Urban regions, notably Los Angeles and San Francisco, were once again inundated, causing serious damage to houses, businesses, and transit networks. Floodwaters devastated crops and livestock in the Central Valley, further devastating the agricultural industry.

The monsoon season brought heavy rains to Arizona, which was already suffering from high temperatures. Rapid runoff from parched soil caused flash floods in cities such as Phoenix and Tucson. Rural areas, particularly those near washes and rivers, were severely flooded, causing home and infrastructure damage or destruction. The economic losses were significant, and the recovery was slow and costly.

Similar patterns emerged in New Mexico, with heavy rains causing post-wildfire flooding in recently burned areas. The bare and charred soil from the wildfires was unable to absorb rain, resulting in rapid runoff and flash floods.

Communities near wildfire scars, such as those in the Santa Fe National Forest, have once again seen significant flooding. Floodwaters carrying ash and debris damaged or destroyed roads, bridges, and residences. The floods also contaminated water supplies, complicating the recovery efforts for affected towns. The economic toll was high, particularly in rural communities that relied on agriculture and tourism.

In the southeastern United States, Florida continued to deal with the combined effects of king tides and hurricane-induced flooding. In 2024, Miami had many king tide events, during which the highest tides of the year flooded low-lying streets, interrupting daily life and business operations. The regular flooding caused by king tides resulted in significant economic losses and deteriorating property prices in flood-prone communities. In addition to king tides, the 2024 hurricane season saw numerous intense storms that produced widespread flooding in Miami and other coastal locations. These disasters highlighted the city's susceptibility to harsh weather and the importance of effective resilience planning.

The reaction to these occurrences has required substantial coordination across federal, state, and local entities. Emergency services have been stretched thin as they provide help and undertake rescue operations in flood-affected areas. Shelters have been created to assist displaced residents, and rehabilitation activities continue. The economic impact of these floods has been significant, with insurance claims and property losses totaling billions of dollars.

Following these recent incidents, there has been a renewed emphasis on upgrading infrastructure and community resilience to deal with the growing threat of extreme weather. California is investing heavily in levee upgrades, drainage system improvements, and the development of more effective water management plans. The state is also concentrating on long-term climate adaptation methods, such as rebuilding natural floodplains and wetlands to absorb floodwaters and mitigate the impact of such occurrences.

Arizona is improving its flood management systems, which include stronger drainage infrastructure and flood control methods. Public awareness initiatives are underway to educate citizens about the dangers of flash floods and the significance of disaster preparedness. Efforts are also being made to improve vegetation and soil management practices to increase water absorption and prevent runoff following heavy rainfall.

New Mexico is researching ways to address post-wildfire flood concerns, such as early warning systems and better land management practices. Efforts are continuing to recover plants in burned areas, which will help stabilize the soil and decrease erosion. Community preparedness initiatives are being created to educate residents on the dangers of post-wildfire floods and the significance of disaster planning.

Miami is making significant investments in infrastructure to combat flooding, such as leveling roadways, building pumps, and improving the stormwater drainage system. The city is also looking into novel solutions, such as erecting sea barriers and developing green infrastructure to absorb and manage floodwaters. Public education campaigns regarding flood dangers, the significance of flood insurance, and evacuation planning are among the initiatives aimed at increasing community resilience. Miami is also changing construction standards and land-use plans to better prepare for future floods.

Overall, the events of 2024 have underlined the critical need for comprehensive climate adaptation and resilience plans in the United States. The rising frequency and intensity of heatwaves and floods highlight the impact of climate change and the importance of coordinating efforts to reduce these hazards. These techniques rely heavily on improved prediction models, infrastructure, and community readiness. States that invest in these sectors can better safeguard their citizens and businesses from the devastation caused by extreme weather.

CHAPTER 7

Impact on Ecosystems And Biodiversity

Effects Of Heatwaves On Flora And Fauna

Heatwaves can significantly impact ecosystems and biodiversity. These extreme weather events can cause significant stress in both plant and animal species, affecting their physiological processes, habits, and survival rates.

FLORA

Plants are especially sensitive to temperature changes. During a heatwave, the increased temperature can hasten evaporation rates, resulting in more water loss from soil and vegetation. This process, known as evapotranspiration, can lead to severe drought conditions, compounding the burden on plant populations.

One direct effect of heatwaves on flora is wilting and, in severe situations, plant death. Species that are not acclimated to high temperatures may incur physiological stress, resulting in reduced photosynthetic activity. Photosynthesis is essential for plant development and energy production, and its suppression can result in stunted growth, lower reproductive success, and, eventually, plant mortality.

Heatwaves can also affect plant phenology, or the timing of developmental processes like blooming, fruiting, and leaf shedding. For example, prolonged heat can produce early or delayed flowering, which affects pollination and seed production. This disruption has the potential to have a domino impact on ecosystems since plants play an important role in supplying food and habitat for a variety of animals.

FAUNA

Heatwaves have a tremendous effect on animals. Many species require precise temperature ranges to survive. When temperatures exceed these limits, animals may experience heat stress, dehydration, and, in the worst-case scenario, death.

Mammals and birds are especially vulnerable to heatwaves. Heatwaves, for example, have been linked to higher bird mortality rates. Birds with high metabolic rates may struggle to locate enough food and water amid intense heat, resulting in fatigue and death. Heatwaves can also cause birds to abandon their nests, leading to the loss of eggs and chicks.

Heatwaves can also be harmful to reptiles and amphibians, who rely on external heat sources to regulate their body temperature. Excessive heat can cause hyperthermia, driving these animals to seek cooler microhabitats. This activity may impair their capacity to forage, mate, and perform other critical functions.

Heatwaves have an impact on aquatic habitats as well. Elevated water temperatures can reduce dissolved oxygen levels in bodies of water, putting fish and other aquatic animals under stress. Fish kills are common during heat waves, especially in shallow or slow-moving environments where oxygen levels can drop rapidly.

INDIRECT EFFECTS

Heatwaves can also have an indirect impact on flora and wildlife by modifying habitat quality and availability. For example, prolonged heat can cause wildfires, destroying vegetation and altering landscapes. These fires can cause both immediate and long-term changes in habitat structure, influencing the availability of food and shelter for a variety of animals.

Furthermore, heatwaves can affect species interactions. Heatwaves, for example, may disrupt the timing of blooming and pollinator activity patterns, causing plants and pollinators to become disoriented. Similarly, predator-prey dynamics can be influenced if one species tolerates heat better than another.

Effects of Flooding on Natural Habitats

Flooding, a natural hydrological phenomenon, has a significant impact on ecosystem structure. While regular floods are necessary to sustain the health and diversity of many habitats, major flooding events, which are frequently worsened by climate change, can have devastating effects on natural habitats and the species they support.

1. Riverine and waterlogged ecosystems

Flooding is a normal and beneficial event in riverine and wetland environments. Seasonal rain restores soil nutrients, promotes aquatic plant growth, and serves as breeding grounds for a variety of fish and amphibians. However, catastrophic floods can overwhelm these systems, destroying habitat and causing significant biodiversity loss.

Extreme floods in riverine systems can destroy riverbanks, changing the course of rivers and displacing plant and animal populations. Increased turbidity and sediment load can cause harm to aquatic plants and restrict light penetration, inhibiting photosynthesis. In addition, the rapid flow of floodwaters may displace or kill fish and invertebrates.

Extreme flooding can also have a significant impact on wetlands, which rely on a precise balance of water levels. Excessive water can drown plants, reducing plant diversity. This, in turn, impacts the entire food web, as many animal species rely on marsh plants for food and shelter. Disruption of wetland habitats can result in population decreases of birds, amphibians, and other species that rely on them.

2. Terrestrial habitats

Flooding can have a significant impact on terrestrial environments, especially in locations not often exposed to high water levels. Extreme flooding can cause soil erosion, loss of vegetation, and changes in soil composition. These changes have the potential to alter the structure and function of terrestrial ecosystems, affecting plant and animal groups alike.

Flooding has an especially devastating impact on forests and grasslands. Floodwaters can uproot trees, wash away soil, and deposit debris, changing the landscape. Vegetation loss can cause erosion and sedimentation in downstream water bodies, further affecting aquatic ecosystems. Disruption of these environments can move species, diminish food availability, and alter predator-prey relationships.

3. Coastal ecosystems

Coastal ecosystems, such as mangroves, salt marshes, and estuaries, are prone to flooding, especially during storm surges and harsh weather. These ecosystems serve an important role in preventing coastal erosion, providing habitat for a variety of species, and supporting fisheries.

Extreme floods can inundate coastal ecosystems with saltwater, changing salinity levels and impacting plant and animal life. Mangroves and salt marshes, which are acclimated to precise salinity ranges, may die off if subjected to protracted or extreme flooding. The loss of these ecosystems may limit the availability of nursery grounds for fish and other marine organisms.

Furthermore, floods can introduce contaminants and nutrients into coastal habitats, causing water quality issues like hypoxia (low oxygen levels) and toxic algal blooms. These conditions can exacerbate the stress on marine life, resulting in population decreases of fish and other aquatic animals.

I. Indirect effects

Flooding can also have an indirect impact on ecosystems by changing the availability of resources and habitat connectivity. For example, the deposition of nutrient-rich sediments can encourage the spread of invasive plant species, which can outcompete local flora and destroy biodiversity. Flooding can split ecosystems, isolating populations and limiting genetic diversity, raising the danger of local extinction.

Furthermore, floods can cause species displacement, which can alter species interactions and community dynamics. If animals are forced into smaller, less suitable environments, predators may have a harder time finding food, and competition for resources may intensify

Synergistic Effects On Ecosystems

Heatwaves and flooding can have a synergistic effect, exacerbating the impacts on ecosystems and biodiversity. These combined stressors can have more severe and complex environmental impacts than either stressor alone.

1. Compound stress on flora and fauna.

Heatwaves and flooding can occur in close succession, causing severe stress for many animals. For example, plants that survive a heatwave may be damaged and more vulnerable to subsequent flooding. Plants with lower vigor may be unable to recover, resulting in greater mortality rates and long-term decreases in plant populations.

Similarly, animals exposed to heat waves may suffer from dehydration, decreased food availability, and increased predation danger. If these animals are then exposed to flooding, their weakened status may limit their capacity to flee or seek refuge, increasing fatality rates. The combined impacts of heat stress and flood-induced displacement can lower reproductive success and change population dynamics.

2. Altered ecosystem processes

Heatwaves and flooding can also combine to affect important ecological processes such as nitrogen cycling, decomposition, and primary productivity. For example, heatwaves can accelerate the decomposition of organic materials, releasing nutrients into the soil. However, future flooding can remove these minerals, lowering soil fertility and impairing plant growth.

Heatwaves in aquatic ecosystems can raise water temperatures, lower dissolved oxygen levels, and stress aquatic life. Flooding can then introduce new stresses, such as increased turbidity and silt, lowering water quality and harming aquatic life. Heat and flooding can cause a shift in species composition, with more tolerant species replacing less adapted ones.

3. Habitat alteration and fragmentation

Heatwaves combined with flooding have the potential to significantly modify and fragment habitats. Heatwaves can trigger wildfires, destroying vegetation and leaving open, naked places. Flooding can then erode these places, altering the terrain and limiting animal mobility. Loss of habitat connectivity can isolate populations, lowering genetic diversity and increasing the likelihood of local extinctions.

Furthermore, the combination of heatwaves and flooding might facilitate the spread of exotic species. Heat stress may make native species less competitive, allowing invasive species to establish and spread more easily. Floodwaters can also disseminate invasive plant seeds and propagules, allowing them to spread further.

4. Safety and adaptation

Understanding the mutual consequences of heatwaves and flooding is crucial for building successful conservation and management plans. Adaptive management approaches can improve ecosystem resilience, which is the ability to rebound from shocks. For example, restoring natural floodplains and wetlands can help absorb floodwaters and mitigate the effects of extreme weather events. Protecting and improving vegetation cover can also assist to reduce the effects of heatwaves by providing shade and lowering soil temperatures.

Climate change may increase the frequency and intensity of heatwaves and flooding, therefore adaptive management solutions should take this into account. Climate projections can help conservationists design more rigorous strategies to safeguard ecosystems and biodiversity.

In summary,

The combined consequences of heatwaves and flooding pose considerable threats to ecosystems and biodiversity. These coupled pressures can lead to more serious and complicated ecological impacts, highlighting the need for comprehensive and integrated approaches to environmental management. Addressing the impacts of these extreme weather events requires coordinated efforts across multiple sectors and levels of governance, from local communities to national policies.

CHAPTER: 8

Human And Socioeconomic

Impacts

Public Health Concerns

Climate change, by amplifying extreme weather events like heat waves and flooding, poses considerable public health risks. These effects are complex, influencing physical health, psychological well-being, and overall community wellness.

Effect Of Heatwaves On Health

Heatwaves pose serious threats to public health. High temperatures can produce heat-related disorders such heat exhaustion, heat rash, and heatstroke, which can be fatal if not treated immediately. Heatwaves put vulnerable people, such as the elderly, small children, and those with pre-existing health concerns, at danger.

Over 70,000 people died as a result of the 2003 European heatwave, one of the deadliest on record. The elderly and people with chronic conditions accounted for the majority of these deaths. Heatwaves also exacerbate respiratory and cardiovascular problems because high temperatures raise ground-level ozone and other pollutants, resulting in poor air quality.

The heat island effect, which occurs when urban temperatures are higher than those in adjacent rural areas due to human activity and infrastructure, can exacerbate the effects of heatwaves. For example, during the 2018 heatwave in the United States, cities like New York and Chicago had much higher temperatures than rural areas, resulting in more hospital admissions for heat-related ailments.

Effect Of Flood On Health

Flooding creates a unique set of public health challenges. Immediate health hazards during floods include injury from fast-moving waters, drowning, and trauma from debris. Flooding can cause outbreaks of waterborne diseases such cholera, dysentery, and leptospirosis as a result of contaminated water supplies. For example, the 2010 floods in Pakistan resulted in a considerable increase in instances of diarrhea and other waterborne infections among the impacted population.

Standing flood waters can also serve as breeding grounds for mosquitoes, increasing the risk of vector-borne illnesses like malaria, dengue fever, and West Nile virus. Hurricane Harvey in 2017, which produced severe flooding in Texas, resulted in an increase in mosquito populations, raising worries about disease transmission.

Extreme weather events also have a significant impact on mental health. The anguish of losing one's home, livelihood, and loved ones can cause anxiety, sadness, and post-traumatic stress disorder (PTSD). Following Hurricane Katrina in 2005, many survivors had long-term mental health challenges, emphasizing the importance of comprehensive mental health treatment in disaster recovery efforts.

Climate Change Impact On Economy

The economic implications of catastrophic weather events caused by climate change are enormous. These costs include direct damage to infrastructure and property, indirect effects on numerous economic sectors, and long-term financial burdens on governments and communities.

Direct damage

Extreme weather can inflict significant direct damage to property and infrastructure. Heatwaves can cause increased energy consumption as people use air conditioning to deal with high temperatures, resulting in higher electricity costs and strain on the electrical grid. During the 2020 California heat wave, rolling blackouts occurred due to high electrical consumption, hurting both companies and homes.

Flooding causes significant damage to homes, businesses, and public infrastructure like roads, bridges, and utilities. The 2019 floods in the Midwest United States cost an estimated $12.5 billion in damage, impacting thousands of houses and agricultural grounds. The costs of repairing and rebuilding following such calamities can put a strain on both public and private finances.

Effect on agriculture

The agriculture sector is especially exposed to the economic consequences of severe weather. Heatwaves can affect crop yields by stressing plants and lowering productivity. For example, the 2012 North American heat wave resulted in severe maize and soybean production losses, raising food prices and causing farmers to lose money.

Flooding can ruin crops, deplete topsoil, and interrupt planting and harvesting schedules. The 2011 Thailand floods, which were among the most expensive in terms of agricultural impact, flooded wide swaths of farmland, resulting in significant losses in rice production and influencing the world rice market.

Impact On Infrastructure

The increasing frequency and severity of extreme weather events have significant implications for the insurance industry. Insurance claims related to natural disasters have skyrocketed, leading to higher premiums and, in some cases, making insurance unaffordable or unavailable for high-risk areas. After the 2017 hurricanes in the Caribbean and the Gulf of Mexico, many insurance companies faced unprecedented payouts, prompting a reevaluation of risk models and premium structures.

Governments frequently face a significant financial burden in the aftermath of climate disaster, rebuilding infrastructure, and supporting affected communities. The Federal Emergency Management Agency (FEMA) in the United States, for example, spends billions annually on disaster response and recovery. These expenses may siphon finances from other essential sectors such as education, healthcare, and infrastructure development.

Impact on infrastructure

Extreme weather events significantly impact infrastructure, disrupting essential services and hindering economic activities. The adaptation of infrastructure systems are important to reducing these effects and sustaining community sustainability.

Transportation systems

Transportation infrastructure, including roads, bridges, railways, and airports, is particularly susceptible to damage from heat waves and flooding. High temperatures can cause asphalt to soften and buckle, creating hazardous driving conditions and requiring costly repairs. During the 2021 Pacific Northwest heatwave, several highways experienced pavement blowouts, disrupting travel and commerce.

Flooding can wash away roads and bridges, isolate communities, and disrupt supply chains. The 2019 floods in the Midwest United States caused extensive damage to transportation networks, delaying the delivery of goods and increasing transportation costs. Railways are also affected, as tracks can be submerged or washed out, leading to delays and increased maintenance costs.

Energy infrastructure

The energy sector faces significant challenges from extreme weather. Heatwaves increase electricity demand for cooling, straining power grids and increasing the risk of blackouts. In 2021, Texas experienced a severe heatwave that led to record electricity consumption, pushing the grid to its limits and resulting in rolling blackouts.

Flooding can damage power plants, substations, and transmission lines, disrupting electricity supply. During Hurricane Sandy in 2012, floodwaters inundated power facilities in New York and New Jersey, leaving millions without power for days and causing substantial economic losses.

Water and sanitation systems

Water infrastructure, including treatment plants, pipelines, and drainage systems, is also vulnerable. Heatwaves can reduce water availability by increasing evaporation rates and demand, leading to water shortages and restrictions. The 2018 Cape Town water crisis, exacerbated by prolonged drought and heat, highlighted the vulnerability of urban water systems to extreme weather.

Flooding can overwhelm drainage systems, contaminate water supplies, and disrupt sewage treatment processes. The 2017 floods in Houston, Texas, caused by Hurricane Harvey, led to widespread contamination of water sources and damage to wastewater treatment facilities, posing significant health risks and requiring extensive repairs.

Community Displacement and Social Effects

The human dimension of climate change impacts is perhaps most poignantly felt in the displacement of communities and the broader social effects that ensue. Extreme weather events often force people to leave their homes, sometimes permanently, leading to significant social and economic upheaval.

Displacement

Flooding and heat waves can displace large numbers of people. Flooding, in particular, can render homes uninhabitable, forcing residents to seek shelter elsewhere. After Hurricane Katrina in 2005, over a million people were displaced, many of whom faced long-term relocation challenges. The resulting diaspora had profound social and economic impacts on both the displaced individuals and the communities that absorbed them.

Heatwaves can also lead to displacement, particularly in areas where prolonged high temperatures make living conditions unbearable. During the 2015 Indian heatwave, many people were forced to migrate from rural areas to cities in search of cooler conditions and better access to healthcare and resources.

Social Inequality

Extreme weather events often exacerbate existing social inequalities. Vulnerable populations, including low-income communities, minorities, and those with limited access to resources, are disproportionately affected. These groups may have fewer means to prepare for, respond to, and recover from extreme weather events.

For example, during the 2020 California wildfires, lower-income communities faced greater challenges in evacuating and finding temporary shelter compared to wealthier residents. The same is true for heatwaves, where access to air conditioning and healthcare can be a matter of life and death. In urban areas, poorer neighborhoods often lack green spaces and cooling infrastructure, making them more susceptible to the heat island effect.

Psychological And Social Effects

The psychological impacts of extreme weather events are significant and often long-lasting. The trauma of experiencing a disaster, losing homes and loved ones, and the uncertainty of the future can lead to mental health issues such as anxiety, depression, and PTSD. After the 2011 Tōhoku earthquake and tsunami in Japan, many survivors reported long-term psychological distress, highlighting the need for mental health support in disaster recovery.

Social cohesion can also be affected. Communities may experience increased tension and conflict as resources become scarce and recovery efforts strain local systems. However, disasters can also foster a sense of solidarity and collective action, as seen in the community responses to the 2017 Grenfell Tower fire in London, where residents and volunteers came together to support those affected.

Long-term Community Adaptability

Building community adaptability is crucial for mitigating the social impacts of extreme weather events. This involves enhancing local capacities to prepare for, respond to, and recover from disasters. Community-based initiatives, such as local emergency response teams, public awareness campaigns, and the development of resilient infrastructure, are essential components of this effort.

Investing in social infrastructure, such as healthcare, education, and housing, can also enhance resilience by addressing the underlying vulnerabilities that make certain populations more susceptible to extreme weather. Ensuring equitable access to resources and opportunities is vital for creating resilient and adaptive communities capable of withstanding the growing impacts of climate change.

In summary

The human and socioeconomic impacts of extreme weather events are profound and multifaceted. From public health concerns to economic costs, infrastructure damage, and community displacement, these impacts highlight the urgent need for comprehensive strategies to enhance resilience and mitigate risks. Understanding these effects in detail allows for better preparation and response, ultimately protecting both human lives and societal stability.

CHAPTER 9

Future Outlook

Predictions For Future Heatwave And Flooding Incidents

As the climate continues to change, the frequency, intensity, and duration of extreme weather events are projected to increase, posing significant challenges for societies. This section provides an in-depth analysis of predictions for future heatwave and flooding incidents, drawing on current climate models and research.

1. Heatwaves: Heatwaves are expected to become more frequent and severe across many regions of the world due to rising global temperatures. Climate models predict that by the mid-21st century, the average number of days exceeding 35°C (95°F) could increase substantially, particularly in mid-latitude and tropical regions.

For instance, the Intergovernmental Panel on Climate Change (IPCC) projects that under a high-emissions scenario (RCP8.5), the number of extreme heat days could increase by more than 100 days per year in some regions by the 21st century. Even under a moderate-emissions scenario (RCP4.5), significant increases in heatwave frequency and intensity are anticipated.

In the United States, areas like the Southwest, including states such as Arizona, California, and Nevada, are likely to experience the most significant increases in heat wave activity. Urban areas will continue to be particularly vulnerable due to the urban heat island effect, where concrete and asphalt absorb and retain heat, exacerbating high temperatures.

Moreover, nights are expected to become warmer, reducing the natural cooling that typically occurs after sunset. This trend poses additional health risks, as continuous exposure to high temperatures without relief can lead to heat-related illnesses and increase mortality rates.

2. Flooding: Flooding incidents are also expected to become more frequent and severe due to several factors influenced by climate change, including increased precipitation intensity, sea-level rise, and more intense tropical cyclones.

3. Increased precipitation intensity:

Climate models indicate that warming temperatures will lead to an increase in the intensity of heavy rainfall events. Warmer air holds more moisture, which can lead to more substantial and intense precipitation when atmospheric conditions trigger rainfall. This is particularly concerning for regions that are already prone to heavy rainfall and flash flooding.

For example, the Midwest and Northeast United States are projected to see significant increases in the frequency and intensity of heavy rainfall events. The National Climate Assessment suggests that by the late 21st century, the heaviest 1% of rain events are expected to become more intense, leading to higher risks of flooding.

4. Sea-Level rise: Sea-level rise, driven by the thermal expansion of seawater and melting ice sheets and glaciers, will exacerbate coastal flooding risks. Low-lying coastal areas, including major cities like Miami, New York, and New Orleans, face heightened risks of both tidal and storm surge flooding.

The IPCC projects that global mean sea levels could rise by 0.43 to 0.84 meters (1.4 to 2.8 feet) by 2100 under high-emissions scenarios. This rise will significantly increase the frequency and extent of coastal flooding during high tides and storm events. For instance, what was once a rare flooding event (occurring once per century) could become an annual occurrence in many coastal regions.

5. Tropical cyclones: Climate change is expected to influence the intensity of tropical cyclones (hurricanes and typhoons), with a greater proportion of storms reaching higher intensity levels. While the overall number of tropical cyclones may not increase, the storms that do form are likely to produce more rainfall and stronger winds.

Regions like the Gulf Coast and the Eastern Seaboard of the United States are particularly vulnerable to the impacts of more intense tropical cyclones. The increased rainfall associated with these storms will enhance the risk of inland flooding, while stronger storm surges will heighten coastal flooding risks.

Strategies On How To Prepare For Climate Change

Climate change preparedness necessitates a multidimensional approach that includes initiatives for mitigation, adaptation, and resilience development. These tactics include actions taken at the individual, community, national, and global levels.

1.   Mitigation: Mitigation measures seek to reduce greenhouse gas emissions and limit the impact of climate change.

Key mitigation measures include:

I. Transition to renewable energy: The transition from fossil fuels to renewable energy sources, including solar, wind, and hydroelectric power, is critical for lowering carbon emissions. Governments and corporations can encourage the use of renewable energy by providing subsidies, tax breaks, and financing for research and development.

II. Energy efficiency: Improving energy efficiency in buildings, transportation, and industry can result in large emissions reductions. Policies and regulations that encourage energy-saving technology and practices, such as tougher building rules and fuel efficiency standards, are critical.

III. Sustainable agriculture and forestry: Implementing sustainable agricultural practices such as precision farming, agroforestry, and soil conservation can help reduce agricultural emissions. Protecting and rebuilding forests through reforestation and afforestation can help to improve carbon sequestration.

IV. Carbon pricing: Carbon pricing methods, such as carbon taxes or cap-and-trade systems, can promote emissions reductions by putting a price on carbon emissions. Programs for renewable energy and adaptation can receive the revenues from carbon pricing.

V. Adaptation: Adaptation techniques seek to strengthen the resilience of communities and ecosystems to the effects of climate change. The key adaptation measures are:

VI. Infrastructure: Upgrading infrastructure to withstand extreme weather events is critical for protecting people and property. This includes constructing flood barriers, modifying structures to resist heat waves and storms, and strengthening drainage systems.

VII. Water management: Effective water management strategies are critical for dealing with shifts in precipitation patterns and water availability. This includes developing water storage and distribution systems, encouraging water conservation, and adopting integrated water resource management.

VIII. Agricultural adaptation: Developing climate-resilient crops, diversifying agricultural practices, and increasing irrigation efficiency can all help farmers adapt to shifting weather conditions. Financial and technical assistance for farmers can improve their ability to employ adaptive methods.

IX. Community-based adaptation: Engaging local populations in adaptation planning and decision-making can help to ensure that adaptation strategies are culturally suitable and locally relevant. Community-based adaptation projects can boost social cohesiveness and enable residents to take constructive action.

2. BUILDING ADAPTABILITY : Building adaptability means increasing the ability of individuals, communities, and systems to tolerate and recover from climatic shocks.

Important adaptability building strategies include:

I. Early warning system: Creating and deploying early warning systems for extreme weather events can help save lives and reduce damage by providing timely information and allowing for proactive steps. These systems should be accessible and user-friendly for all communities.

II. Disaster risk reduction: Integrating catastrophe risk reduction into development planning and policy frameworks is critical for increasing resilience. This includes identifying and eliminating vulnerabilities, strengthening risk assessments, and creating complete disaster response plans. Disaster risk reduction can be integrated into many sectors of development, allowing society to better prepare for and minimize the effects of catastrophic weather events.

III. Ecosystem-based adaptation: Protecting and restoring natural ecosystems can bring large resilience gains. Healthy ecosystems, such as wetlands, woodlands, and mangroves, can serve as natural weather buffers, lowering the danger of flooding, storm surges, and heat waves. Ecosystem-based adaptation promotes biodiversity and improves ecosystem services like water purification and carbon sequestration. Social protection systems:

Strengthening social protection mechanisms, such as social safety nets, health insurance, and unemployment compensation, can help vulnerable communities become more strong. These networks can provide financial and social support during and after catastrophic weather events, allowing people and communities to recover faster.

IV. Education and capacity-building: Educating people about climate change and its consequences is critical to building resilience. This involves incorporating climate change teaching into school curricula, launching public awareness campaigns, and training experts in fields like agriculture, health, and urban planning. Capacity-building efforts can enable individuals and communities to make informed decisions to safeguard themselves and their surroundings.

V. Policy and governance: Effective policy and governance frameworks are essential for implementing and maintaining climate resilience initiatives. The key policy and governance measures are:

VI. Climate Action Plan: Creating and implementing comprehensive climate action plans at the local, regional, and national levels can help guide and coordinate efforts to mitigate and adapt to climate change. These strategies should establish clear objectives, prioritize tasks, and provide resources for implementation.

VII. Integrative Planning: Climate change considerations can be integrated into many elements of planning and decision-making, including urban planning, land use, transportation, and infrastructure development, to improve resilience. This comprehensive approach ensures that climate hazards are addressed in all development efforts.

VIII. Stakeholder engagement: Climate resilience strategies can be more effective when a diverse variety of stakeholders, including government agencies, corporations, non-governmental organizations, and local communities, are involved in their development and implementation. Inclusive and participatory processes take into account a variety of views and requirements.

IX. International cooperation: Climate change is a worldwide issue that necessitates international cooperation. Countries must collaborate to share information, technologies, and resources, as well as create and implement global agreements and frameworks like the Paris Agreement. International collaboration can also help underdeveloped countries create capacity and provide financial assistance, as they are frequently the most vulnerable to climate consequences.

3. TECHNOLOGICAL INNOVATIONS

Technological innovation is critical to combating climate change and increasing resilience.

The key technological solutions are:

I. Renewable energy technology: Advances in renewable energy technology, such as solar, wind, and geothermal power, are critical for lowering greenhouse gasses. Continued Innovation can boost the efficiency and affordability of these technologies, making them more accessible and widely adopted.

II. Climate adaptability Infrastructure: Developing and deploying climate-resilient infrastructure innovations, such as permeable pavements, green roofs, and upgraded building materials, can help cities better endure extreme weather events. Smart infrastructure solutions, which utilize sensors and data analytics to monitor and control infrastructure in real time, can also boost resilience.

III.   Agricultural   technologies: Drought-resistant crops, precision farming, and sustainable irrigation systems are examples of agricultural technological innovations that can assist farmers in adapting to changing climate circumstances. These technologies can boost production, minimize resource use, and increase food security.

IV. early warning and monitoring systems: Advances in early warning and monitoring technologies, such as satellite remote sensing, weather forecasting, and climate modeling, can help us predict and respond to extreme weather events. These systems can provide real-time and precise information, allowing for preventive measures to protect people and property.

4. COMMUNITY AND INDIVIDUAL ACTIONS: Individuals and communities are crucial in developing resilience to climate change. The *key actions at the community and individual levels are:*

I. Sustainable practices: Adopting sustainable behaviors in daily life, such as decreasing energy and water usage, eliminating trash, and using public transportation, can help reduce environmental impacts and improve climate resilience. Community initiatives, such as community gardens and local recycling programs, can help to enhance sustainability and resilience.

II. Community-based adaptation initiatives: Participating in community-based adaptation efforts, such as restoring natural habitats, constructing community shelters, and creating local emergency plans, can boost community resilience. These initiatives can boost social cohesion and enable communities to take collaborative action.

III. Advocating and education: Advocating for climate action and educating people on the value of resilience can lead to positive change. Individuals can engage with lawmakers, advocate for climate-friendly policies, and raise awareness through education and outreach campaigns.

IV. Emergency preparedness: Individual and community resilience can be increased by making family emergency plans, preparing emergency supplies, and staying up-to-date on local threats and response strategies. Emergency drills and understanding how to contact emergency services are also vital.

In summary

Preparing for climate change necessitates a comprehensive and multifaceted approach that encompasses mitigation, adaptation, and resilience-building methods. Societies can better endure and recover from the effects of climate change by lowering greenhouse gas emissions, strengthening infrastructure and community resilience, and encouraging innovation and cooperation. Addressing climate change is a shared duty that necessitates concerted

efforts at all levels, from individuals to governments, to create a more sustainable and resilient future.

Conclusion

Summary Of Findings

A thorough analysis of climate change implications in the United States demonstrates an urgent need for action and adaptation. The study's major findings highlight the increasing frequency and intensity of extreme weather events like heat waves and flooding, which pose serious dangers to both human and natural systems.

Heatwaves have become increasingly frequent and powerful, especially in the southwestern United States. Rising temperatures have a negative impact not just on human health and mortality rates but also on energy and water supplies. Case studies from Arizona (2023) and California (2022) demonstrate the devastating effects of extreme heat waves on public health, infrastructure, and ecosystems.

Flooding is also becoming more common, caused by rising sea levels and greater precipitation intensity. The thorough evaluations of flooding events, such as the California atmospheric river flooding in 2023, the Arizona monsoon floods in 2022, and the recurring flooding in Miami caused by king tides and storms, demonstrate the diversity and scope of these hazards. Flooding has far-reaching and complex consequences for infrastructure, human health, and natural environments.

The link between heat waves and flooding is clear in how heat waves contribute to soil hardening and runoff dynamics, increasing flood risk. Heatwaves have an even greater impact on weather patterns, complicating flood prediction and management.

The regional concentration on the southwestern United States, which includes Arizona, California, Nevada, New Mexico, Utah, Colorado, and Texas, as well as the southeastern state of Florida (Miami), provides a thorough understanding of each state's unique issues. Heatwave and flood disasters in these states highlight the importance of specific adaptation and mitigation efforts.

Major heatwave and flooding events, such as the California 2023 heatwave that resulted in atmospheric river flooding, Arizona's 2022 monsoon floods caused by high heat, and New Mexico's post-wildfire flooding in 2022, demonstrate the compound nature of climate impacts. Miami's king tides and hurricane-induced flooding highlight the specific issues that coastal cities face.

Heatwaves and flooding have had a devastating impact on ecosystems and biodiversity, affecting natural habitats and endangering flora and fauna populations. The synergistic effects of these extreme weather events place an additional burden on ecosystems, with long-term implications for biodiversity.

The human and social consequences are significant, with public health problems, economic losses, infrastructure destruction, and community displacement being key difficulties. The economic cost of rebuilding and repairing after extreme weather events, combined with the social consequences of displacement and disruption, emphasizes the importance of comprehensive resilience planning.

Heatwave and flooding incidents are expected to become more frequent and severe in the future. Long-term climate change projections indicate considerable changes in temperature, precipitation patterns, and sea levels. Strategies to prepare for these changes include both mitigation and adaptation strategies, with a focus on sustainable behaviors, technological innovation, and strong policy frameworks.

Final Thoughts On Combating Climate Change In The United States

Addressing climate change in the United States necessitates a comprehensive strategy that combines mitigation to reduce greenhouse gas emissions with adaptation to manage the effects of a changing climate. The outcomes of this study emphasize the critical necessity for comprehensive and coordinated actions at all levels of society.

Mitigation initiatives must prioritize lowering carbon emissions through the use of renewable energy sources, increasing energy efficiency, and encouraging sustainable land use practices. Policies that promote the transition to a low-carbon economy are critical to accomplishing these objectives.

Adaptation techniques must be adapted to the unique vulnerabilities and needs of each location. For example, in the southern United States, where heat waves are a serious concern, improvements to cooling systems and water management are critical. In coastal areas such as Miami, upgrading flood barriers and executing managed retreat plans are critical to safeguarding populations from increasing sea levels and storm surges.

Building resilience entails investing in infrastructure that can endure catastrophic weather events, preserving and restoring natural ecosystems that serve as buffers, and improving social protection systems to assist vulnerable communities. Education and community participation are critical components of resilience building, allowing individuals and communities to take proactive steps.

Policy and governance are crucial to solving climate change. Effective policies that include climate issues in all phases of planning and development are required to ensure long-term sustainability. International collaboration and adherence to global agreements, such as the Paris Agreement, are also critical in tackling the global character of climate change.

Technological innovation will be critical in mitigating and adapting to climate change. Continued research and development in renewable energy, climate-resilient infrastructure, and early warning systems can help us better manage climate hazards.

Finally, individual and community efforts are critical for tackling climate change. Sustainable lifestyle choices, community-based adaptation programs, and lobbying for climate-friendly policies all help to create a path against climate change in the future.

In summary

The route forward necessitates a comprehensive and multifaceted approach that harnesses the capabilities and resources of all sectors of society. By combining mitigation, adaptation, resilience-building, and innovative solutions, the United States can effectively address climate change concerns and move toward a more sustainable and secure a future for everyone.

www.ingramcontent.com/pod-product-compliance
Lightning Source LLC
Chambersburg PA
CBHW061633250726
48659CB00004B/1202